THE LIONS' DEN:

FACING YOURS

PRESTON PARRISH

AWAKENINGS, INCORPORATED
Winston-Salem, North Carolina

THE LIONS' DEN: FACING YOURS

Unless otherwise noted, Scripture quotations are taken from the New American Standard Bible, © 1960, 1962, 1963, 1968, 1971, 1972, 1973, 1975, 1977 by The Lockman Foundation. Used by permission.

Cover design: Marsha S. Thrift, Graphic Designer

Printed in the United States of America

ISBN 0-9633470-8-x

Library of Congress Catalog Card Number: 92-72324

Published by *AWAKENINGS, INCORPORATED*, Post Office Box 25251, Winston-Salem, NC 27114.

Be of sober spirit, be on the alert. Your adversary, the devil, prowls about like a roaring lion, seeking someone to devour. But resist him, firm in your faith, knowing that the same experiences of suffering are being accomplished by your brethren who are in the world.

1 Peter 5:8,9 NASB

THE LIONS' DEN: FACING YOURS

Contents

Preface

I am a disciple of Jesus Christ.

That statement says as much about some other people I have been privileged to know as it does about me, for according to the Great Commission in Matthew 28:19, disciples are "made."

In other words, every follower of Jesus Christ is a product of the spiritual labor of others—of people who pray and demonstrate God's love, who verbally share the message of the Gospel, and who provide teaching and nurture once Christ is received.

Therefore, the fact that I am a disciple of Christ is a testimony to the faithfulness of numerous other Christians who have invested in me over the years, in order to help me grow and mature spiritually.

This book too is a testimony to the people who have invested in me. Along the way, many individuals have shared God's Word with me, and most (if not all) of any insights I can relate today were probably introduced to me by someone else.

Of course, all of us who are taught God's Word are to be "examining the Scriptures daily, to see whether these things [are] so" (Acts 17:11). God the Holy Spirit is our ultimate Teacher, who "will guide [us] into all the truth" (John 16:13).

Many, though, could rightly claim ownership of the

material which follows—not because I have intention-
ally made unattributed use of anyone else's work, but
because the body of truth which comprises our Christian faith is continuously being received . . . then
imparted . . . again and again and again.

That's the way God designed it to work. In reality,
He deserves the credit for anything which is good in
this book, because He is "the Author and Perfecter of
faith" (Hebrews 12:2). I deserve the blame for all which
isn't.

As you read, please be generous with your praise of
Him, and be merciful in your criticism of me. While He
Himself is indeed perfect, I am not. I'm still on the way
toward conformity to His image, and many days I feel
that I've barely begun making progress in that direction.

My personal appreciation is hereby expressed to all
who have had a part in the production of this book, and
to all who have encouraged and supported me, my wife
Glenda, and our children Hannah, Gregory and Nathan
in our lives and ministry. My specific prayer as this
book is released is that Hannah, Gregory and Nathan
will become spiritually strong and courageous—like
Daniel—for the eternal glory of our Lord and Savior
Jesus Christ.

Preston Parrish
September, 1992

 # **Introduction**

Writing this book was not high on my agenda. Lots of other responsibilities were clamoring for my attention. I have a family to nurture, a golden retriever to clean up after, a backyard garden with weeds, a car that needs fixing, letters to write, bills to pay . . . sound familiar?

Yet as I studied the Old Testament Book of Daniel, dwelling especially on the account in chapter six of his experience in the lions' den, I felt compelled to share some of the thoughts which came to me.

Daniel in the lions' den—the story captured my imagination the first time I heard it as a small boy at bedtime. For years, though, it seemed to be a quaint bit of Bible history which had little relevance to my life. I was wrong.

As an adult committed to Jesus Christ, I now realize that I can learn some important principles for living from Daniel and the experience he had so long ago. Daniel is a forefather in the faith for all of us who believe during these waning days of the twentieth century. He clashed with the values and ways of his world, and as we seek to live faithfully, we will too. We can benefit greatly by reflecting on the life of this man whom the angel Gabriel declared to be "highly esteemed" (Daniel 9:23).

The events recorded in the sixth chapter of Daniel are a concentrated vein of pure gold in the motherlode of the Scriptures, just waiting to enrich all who would mine it for themselves. I felt somehow that many others—perhaps you—need the encouragement and instruction to be found there.

Daniel wound up between a rock and the "king of the beasts" because his allegiance to God put him at odds with his idolatrous world. In a profound way, though he lived 600 years before Christ appeared, Daniel modeled the relationship with God which the Apostle Paul wrote about in Philippians 3:7-11, and which is to be the experience of every believer today:

> *But whatever things were gain to me, those things I have counted as loss for the sake of Christ. More than that, I count all things to be loss in view of the surpassing value of knowing Christ Jesus my Lord, for whom I have suffered the loss of all things, and count them but rubbish in order that I may gain Christ . . . that I may know Him, and the power of His resurrection and the fellowship of His sufferings, being conformed to His death; in order that I may attain to the resurrection from the dead.*

So, it's fair to say I've written what follows not because I wanted to, but because I had to, in order to build up my brothers and sisters in Christ. Many Christians today are in situations which can be considered their own personal "lions' dens"—some at work or school, others even in their family or church. If that's you, read on. Hopefully the Lord will use what follows to strengthen and help you.

If that's not you, read on anyway. Sooner or later, you'll find yourself in a "lions' den" you may never have expected to visit, and now is the time to prepare. When that day comes, you'll find out for yourself (if you don't know it already), that the lions' den is no resort hotel.

Preston Parrish
Winston-Salem, North Carolina

May I Show You To Your Room?

Step One: Commitment to Holiness

Hotels and motels are fun places for kids.

Family vacations during my childhood often found us pulling into the parking lot of a motel at the end of a long day of driving. My father would go into the office to rent rooms for the night. After what seemed like forever, he would emerge carrying our room keys. My restless brother and I could hardly wait to get out of the car (neither could my mother!) and explore our new surroundings.

Color TVs, ice and drink machines, the restaurant, and most important, the swimming pool—all of these fascinated two energetic boys on summer break from school. I used to think it would be great if I could live my whole life in a hotel.

Many years have passed since then. I've spent more nights than I care to count in hotels, motels, and assorted other facilities on six continents. Some offered welcome respite from tiring travels. Others made me wonder how I could have ever wanted to sleep anywhere but home, in my own bed.

Daniel must have longed for his own bed the night he stayed in the lions' den. The way he acquired his hairy, snarling bedfellows is described in the first six chapters of the Old Testament book bearing his name.

Daniel was a Jew who lived in Judah at a time of great turmoil. While he was a youth, his land was conquered by Nebuchadnezzar, king of Babylon (now known as Iraq); Nebuchadnezzar carried the Jews, including young Daniel, into exile. God allowed this fate to befall His chosen people because they had repeatedly rebelled against Him. Time after time, they showed by their disobedience that they preferred the idolatrous ways of their pagan neighbors over devotion to the one true God. God had sent prophets to warn His people of the approaching judgement, but they did not listen. Finally, judgement came, and Daniel and his countrymen found themselves captive in a strange place called Babylon.

Just as stars shine most brightly against the darkest night sky, Daniel emerged as a divinely pleasing exception among his wayward kin. His intelligence, abilities and good looks earned him a place in Nebuchadnezzar's officer training school. Three of his friends—Shadrach, Meshach and Abednego—were also selected. For Daniel, his descent into the lions' den began during his training there in Nebuchadnezzar's court.

Wait a minute, you may be thinking. *Daniel was thrown into the lions' den under Darius half a century later.*

That's right; he didn't actually "check in" till then. In the first days of his exile, though, Daniel—far from home, most likely homesick and heartbroken—took his first steps in that direction.

Step one is recorded in Daniel 1:8:

> *But Daniel made up his mind that he would not defile himself . . .*

The specific issue which prompted Daniel to take this step was a dietary one. He didn't want to eat food that didn't conform to the Law of Moses. Daniel's motivation, however, was that even under the duress of captivity, he believed it was important to honor God in his eating and drinking. He understood what the prophet Isaiah had discovered a century or so earlier:

> *Holy, Holy, Holy, is the Lord of hosts . . .*
> (Isaiah 6:3).

He remembered what the Lord told Moses:

> *Thus you are to be holy to Me, for I the Lord am holy; and I have set you apart from the people to be Mine* (Leviticus 20:26).

It's worth stopping here to ask a question: how committed are you and I to being holy, or totally set apart in our hearts and lives from everything in our world which is contrary to God's perfect character? Holiness is not one of those themes of Christian living on which we tend to dwell. Too often, we Christians conduct ourselves no differently from the people around us who are living for themselves rather than Christ. We sometimes seem to hold identical values and priorities.

Rather than living as individuals "set apart," we often conduct ourselves as if we were called to "blend in."

Daniel certainly didn't blend in. He chose early on to contend for his convictions, even when doing so meant resisting the orders of the most powerful ruler of his day, Nebuchadnezzar. He established at the outset that, if necessary, he would suffer for doing what he knew to be right, rather than compromise.

I recently came across a slogan reading: "In a world of compromise, some people don't." That was true of Daniel.

In Daniel chapter one, he acted in relation to a dietary matter; in Daniel chapter six, the issue involved prayer. In both situations, however, Daniel deemed dishonoring God to be worse than any punishment his captors could inflict upon him. Under different circumstances his actions were shaped by that one principle. So when Daniel chose to ask for a change of menu in Nebuchadnezzar's restaurant, he was taking his first step toward the lions' den.

Had he waited to begin making a stand for God till the trial in chapter six arose, chances are he would not have had the spiritual strength to do it. He did not put it off, though, so by this time he had grown strong.

Our allegiance to God and our witness in the world are like muscle tissue—the more we exercise, the stronger we become. Any good athlete knows that he or she must "work out" consistently in order to achieve peak condition and performance. Let me ask: how strong are you right now? Have you just been "going with the flow" around you, or do you know both the strain and the exhilaration of resisting the world's unholy pressures, in order to honor the one true God?

The Apostle Paul clearly understood how crucial it is to maintain one's spiritual muscle tone, and the admonitions he gave to early Christians still apply to us today:

> *Whether, then, you eat or drink or whatever you do, do all to the glory of God* (1 Corinthians 10:31).

> *I urge you therefore, brethren, by the mercies of God, to present your bodies a living and holy sacrifice, acceptable to God, which is your spiritual service of worship* (Romans 12:1).

If you're feeling a little flabby, spiritually speaking, *now* is the time to start getting into shape. This is one important lesson we learn from Daniel. Many hotels these days have fitness centers with treadmills, weight machines, and other equipment to help guests improve their physical condition. Remember, though, when you check into the lions' den, there won't be any—it's no resort hotel—so you better start now.

May I Show You To Your Room?

Step Two: Commitment to Truth

Just as Daniel took his first step toward the lions' den during Nebuchadnezzar's reign, he took another step in that direction under Nebuchadnezzar's grandson, wicked King Belshazzar. Compared to Nebuchadnezzar, Belshazzar was both self-centered and irreverent.

When Nebuchadnezzar conquered Jerusalem, Daniel 1:2 says he took to Babylon "some of the vessels of the house of God" and put them "in the house of his god." In other words, while Nebuchadnezzar was an idol worshiper, he did show at least a little respect for the religious practices of the people he conquered. By the end of his reign, in response to God's dealings with him, Nebuchadnezzar "blessed the Most High and praised and honored Him who lives forever" (Daniel 4:34). He also declared of Him:

> *For His dominion is an everlasting dominion,*
> *And His kingdom endures from generation to generation.*
> *And all the inhabitants of the earth are accounted as nothing,*

*But He does according to His will in the host of
heaven
And among the inhabitants of earth;
And no one can ward off His hand
Or say to Him, "What hast Thou done?"*
(Daniel 4:34-35).

The last words of Nebuchadnezzar recorded by Daniel
are:

*Now I Nebuchadnezzar praise, exalt, and honor the
King of heaven, for all His works are true and His
ways just, and He is able to humble those who walk
in pride* (Daniel 4:37).

Not a bad ending for the king who at one point in
his life had Daniel's friends—Shadrach, Meshach and
Abednego—thrown into the fiery furnace for refusing
to bow down to his golden image!

Belshazzar, however, was a different story. None of
Nebuchadnezzar's reverence for God took root in his
life. Chapter five of Daniel tells how Belshazzar conducted himself and how he met his end. Especially
significant is the way he partied:

*Belshazzar the king held a great feast for a thousand
of his nobles, and he was drinking wine in the presence of the thousand. When Belshazzar tasted the
wine, he gave orders to bring the gold and silver
vessels which Nebuchadnezzar his father had taken
out of the temple which was in Jerusalem, in order
that the king and his nobles, his wives, and his concubines might drink from them. Then they brought
the gold vessels that had been taken out of the temple,
the house of God which was in Jerusalem; and the
king and his nobles, his wives, and his concubines
drank from them. They drank the wine and praised*

the gods of gold and silver, of bronze, iron, wood, and stone (Daniel 5:1-4).

Wow! Not only did Belshazzar throw a drunken orgy—he used his sensuous feast as an occasion to flout God and defile the vessels which had been created for use in worshiping Him. Nebuchadnezzar never did that!

To understand how offensive this must have been to God, it is important to look back at the Old Testament book of 2 Chronicles where, after Solomon had built and furnished the Temple, God said:

> *I . . . have chosen this place for Myself as a house of sacrifice . . . Now My eyes shall be open and My ears attentive to the prayer offered in this place. For now I have chosen and consecrated this house that My name may be there forever, and My eyes and My heart will be there perpetually* (2 Chronicles 7:1, 15-16).

In other words, even though these vessels from the Temple were now in the possession of Babylon's king far from Jerusalem, God hadn't lost sight of them. As Solomon asserted in Proverbs 15:3:

> *The eyes of the Lord are in every place,*
> *Watching the evil and the good.*

As God watched Belshazzar's feast, He apparently didn't see any good. The king had gone too far, and God gave him the "backhand":

> *Suddenly the fingers of a man's hand emerged and began writing opposite the lampstand on the plaster of the wall of the king's palace, and the king saw the back of the hand that did the writing. Then the king's face grew pale, and his thoughts alarmed*

> *him; and his hip joints went slack, and his knees*
> *began knocking together* (Daniel 5:5-6).

A clue to what must have happened in heaven at this point is given to us in Psalm 2, which describes God's response to the wicked. Look at verse 4:

> *He who sits in the heavens laughs,*
> *The Lord scoffs at them.*

When sensuous, irreverent Belshazzar was "on the ropes" before laughing, scoffing God, Daniel was brought into the picture. In this situation he demonstrated a personal quality which can be viewed as his second step toward the lions' den. King Belshazzar called for his soothsayers to come and read to him the inscription on the wall, promising whoever could do so a purple suit of clothes, a necklace of gold, and a place of authority in his kingdom. Despite this incentive, none of his wise men could read the writing, which caused Belshazzar even greater alarm.

> *. . . his face grew even paler, and his nobles were*
> *perplexed* (Daniel 5:9).

The queen then reminded Belshazzar of Daniel, who had apparently fallen out of favor and lived in obscurity after Nebuchadnezzar died. His reputation survived, though, for the queen (who was most likely Belshazzar's grandmother) said:

> *There is a man in your kingdom in whom is a spirit*
> *of the holy gods; and in the days of your father* [or
> grandfather], *illumination, insight, and wisdom*
> *like the wisdom of the gods were found in him . . .*
> *Let Daniel now be summoned, and he will declare*
> *the interpretation* (Daniel 5:11-12).

Daniel was brought before Belshazzar, informed of the problem, and promised that, if he could interpret the writing, he would receive the reward. Daniel's response represents his second step toward the lions' den:

> *Keep your gifts for yourself, or give your rewards to someone else; however, I will read the inscription to the king and make the interpretation known to him* (Daniel 5:17).

In answering the king as he did, Daniel demonstrated a commitment to declaring God's truth regardless of what he got out of it personally. Whether he profited or suffered made no difference to him—he was going to be straightforward about whatever God revealed to him. Daniel had no way of knowing for sure how the drunken, desperate Belshazzar would respond when Daniel read the message of judgement written on the wall. But he was not going to bend the message to suit the whim of his audience, even if it was a royal one.

Daniel's commitment to being a witness for the truth was his second step toward the lions' den.

In Greek, the root for our English word "witness" is the same one from which we get the word "martyr." Whenever you or I make a commitment to be uncompromising witnesses for God's truth, we are setting our sails for martyrdom, which is not a new experience for Christians.

In the early church, Peter and John got a taste of this fact when their testimony for Christ came to the attention of the Jewish leaders. Peter and John had gone to the Temple to pray; as they approached the gate, a lame man asked them for alms. God used the two apostles to give the man not money, but the ability to walk. His healing caused quite a stir; a crowd gathered and Peter began to preach. Then Peter and John were arrested and introduced to the joys of the Jerusalem jail (it was no resort hotel!).

Next day, Peter and John were brought before all the Jewish rulers, including Caiaphas, who had presided over Christ's trial. The rulers questioned Peter and John, then "commanded them not to speak or teach at all in the name of Jesus" (Acts 4:18).

Peter and John showed themselves to be true descendants of Daniel, however, by declaring:

> *Whether it is right in the sight of God to give heed to you rather than to God, you be the judge; for we cannot stop speaking what we have seen and heard* (Acts 4:19-20).

For the time being, the apostles were released. Later, though, they again found themselves checking into their own personal lions' dens. As an old man, John was banished to lonely exile on the island of Patmos; Peter was crucified upside down. These "witnesses" became "martyrs" because of their unbending commitment to the truth. When you and I make that commitment, we embark on the same course.

The days in which we live are not friendly toward truth. In America, most people worship at the shrine of the open mind. The spirit of our times says, "Believe anything you want, but don't dare tell others that their beliefs may be erroneous." Our world is full of people who, like Pontius Pilate, cynically ask: "What is truth?" (John 18:38).

The age Paul warned Timothy about has come upon us:

> *For the time will come when they will not endure*
> *sound doctrine; but wanting to have their ears*
> *tickled, they will accumulate for themselves teachers*
> *in accordance to their own desires; and will turn*
> *away their ears from the truth, and will turn aside*
> *to myths* (2 Timothy 4:3-4).

The only truth most people are willing to recognize is "what's true for you." That's saddening, because the enemy of truth, Satan, will tickle a person's ears all the way to hell. Jesus said of him:

> *He was a murderer from the beginning, and does*
> *not stand in the truth, because there is no truth in*
> *him. Whenever he speaks a lie, he speaks from his*
> *own nature; for he is a liar, and the father of lies*
> (John 8:44).

In the midst of such an age, it is crucial for us to be steadfast in representing Christ, who said:

> *I am the way, and the truth, and the life; no one*
> *comes to the Father, but through Me* (John 14:6).

The apostles and Daniel certainly "stood" in the truth, and so should we. When we do, though, the lions' den begins coming into view for us. To get there, we—like Daniel—need to take just one more step.

May I Show You To Your Room?

Step Three: Commitment to a Transformed Life

Daniel's third step toward the lions' den occurred during the reign of King Darius, who replaced Belshazzar. Upon coming to power, Darius had the good sense to involve Daniel in administering the kingdom. Judging from the narrative in Daniel chapter six, the two seemed to view one another with affection and respect. Both were older men, well over the age of sixty. Daniel gave Darius every reason to like him:

> *Then this Daniel began distinguishing himself among the commissioners and satraps because he possessed an extraordinary spirit, and the king planned to appoint him over the entire kingdom* (Daniel 6:3).

Then, the inevitable happened. The other commissioners and satraps (assistants to the king) became jealous. Why? Because Daniel's lifestyle was a reproof to them. The excellence with which Daniel conducted himself made their inferior character obvious.

> *Then the commissioners and satraps began trying to*

find a ground of accusation against Daniel in regard to government affairs; but they could find no ground of accusation or evidence of corruption, inasmuch as he was faithful and no negligence or corruption was to be found in him (Daniel 6:4).

After closely scrutinizing Daniel, his rivals concluded that the only way they could prevent his promotion and rid themselves of this pest once and for all was to make his strength—his consistent walk with God—illegal.

We shall not find any ground of accusation against this Daniel unless we find it against him with regard to the law of his God (Daniel 6:5).

Again, it's worth pausing to ask a personal question: can people say that about us? Do we conduct our affairs so that the only fault someone can accuse us of is that we are too close to God? I'm afraid, in my life anyway, that often isn't the case. (If you doubt it, all you have to do is ask my wife and children!)

Written in my Bible, though, beside Daniel 6:5 is a prayer: "Lord, may this be said of me." That prayer hasn't been answered yet, but by the grace of God, it will be one day.

It was true for Daniel, however, so his enemies schemed together and came up with a plan. They proposed to Darius that he issue an irrevocable decree making it a capital offense for prayers to be offered to anyone besides himself. The sentence for violating the law: the lions' den. The plan was no doubt flattering to Darius, and he didn't realize they were trying to harm Daniel rather than honor the king, so Darius agreed.

Finally, the trap was set.

Daniel's foes must have congratulated themselves and rubbed their hands with glee as they anticipated the outcome of their plot. Either Daniel would abide by the law and show himself to be an idolater like the rest of them, or he would disobey and be served to the lions for dinner. Either way, they would be rid of this pest and could continue peacefully living their mediocre lives.

Well, you know the story. Daniel didn't obey the law.

> *Now when Daniel knew that the document was signed, he entered his house (now in his roof chamber he had windows open toward Jerusalem); and he continued kneeling on his knees three times a day, praying and giving thanks before his God, as he had been doing previously. Then these men came by agreement and found Daniel making petition and supplication before his God* (Daniel 6:10-11).

Daniel took his third and final step toward the lions' den by refusing to conform his worship of God to the decrees of men.

God has called you and me to make the same stand. Continuing a passage we began quoting earlier:

> *I urge you therefore, brethren, by the mercies of God, to present your bodies a living and holy sacrifice, acceptable to God, which is your spiritual service of worship. And do not be conformed to this world, but be transformed by the renewing of your mind, that you may prove what the will of God is, that which is good and acceptable and perfect* (Romans 12:1-2).

For Daniel and for us, doing this can be quite dangerous.

The Scripture makes it clear that Daniel knew what the outcome of his action would be. The fact is, to Daniel, it just didn't matter. For him, to live as an idolater would have been worse than facing the lions. Rather, he sought to follow the example of Moses, who

> *refused to be called the son of Pharaoh's daughter;*
> *choosing rather to endure ill-treatment with the*
> *people of God, than to enjoy the passing pleasures of*
> *sin; considering the reproach of Christ greater*
> *riches than the treasures of Egypt; for he was look-*
> *ing to the reward* (Hebrews 11:24-26).

Daniel understood, even though he lived six centuries before Christ appeared, what the Lord Himself declared as prayed on the eve of His own passion:

> *And this is eternal life, that they may know Thee,*
> *the only true God, and Jesus Christ whom Thou*
> *hast sent* (John 17:3).

So Daniel maintained his long-established pattern of spending concentrated time in prayer three times daily. He heeded the words of the Psalmist:

> *As for me, I shall call upon God,*
> *And the Lord will save me.*
> *Evening and morning and at noon, I will complain*
> *and murmur,*
> *And He will hear my voice.*
> *He will redeem my soul in peace from the battle*
> *which is against me,*
> *For they are many who strive with me*
> (Psalm 55:16-18).

It's good to point out that Daniel didn't *start* having his "quiet time" three times daily after Darius' decree was issued. He *continued* doing so, "as he had been doing previously." When the lions' den looms before us, it's too late to start preparing for it. Our spiritual muscles must have been conditioned in advance.

Fortunately, Daniel's knees were accustomed to being on the floor. That's why he was able to take his third step toward the lions' den. That's how Daniel's descendants through the centuries—people like Martin Luther, who launched the Protestant Reformation in the sixteenth century; George Whitefield and John Wesley, who fueled the Great Awakening in the eighteenth century; and Dietrich Bonhoeffer and Corrie ten Boom, who suffered for resisting Adolph Hitler's dictates in the twentieth century—faced the "lions" of their day without flinching. It's what you and I need to practice, as well.

Very honestly, I'm not too impressed with the "organized religion" of our time. Oh, I am an active member in a local church which is part of a so-called mainline denomination. I love the brothers and sisters in Christ there; they are my closest friends. Their prayers, encouragement and help are vital to my family and me. Without them, our lives would be difficult (and lonely) indeed. It is a great privilege to be able to participate in our church's life and ministry, even in a small way.

Ultimately, however, my walk with God—and yours—must be more important to us than even the church and Christian friends we cherish most. Why? Because while the Church with a capital "C"—the Body of Christ—is God's creation and hell itself won't overcome it, the church with a little "c"—in all of its contemporary expressions, variations and imperfections—is indeed temporary.

> ... *when the perfect comes, the partial will be done away* (1 Corinthians 13:10).

If we are content to allow our walk with God merely to conform to what we see around us, we will miss the mark of God's perfection. Do you know the word used in Scripture to convey the idea of "missing the mark"? Sin.

The best local churches, and the best Christian friends, are all like you and me—sinful. We fall short of God's glory as revealed in Jesus Christ. That's why we must focus our eyes on Him, above and beyond the beloved people and traditions in our lives, and "press on toward the goal for the prize of the upward call of God in Christ Jesus" (Philippians 3:14).

Funny thing, though—pressing on toward the upward call often leads us down into the lions' den.

Watch Those Steps

Some time ago, a lodging chain ran an advertising campaign based on the theme: "No surprises, guaranteed!" For weary travelers, they declared, the best surprise when checking into a hotel is *no* surprise. It's better, they asserted, to find your room and everything in it just the way you expect.

As Christians, we really shouldn't be surprised when we find ourselves checking into the lions' den. In fact, it's often possible to anticipate it far in advance.

As I write, summer is approaching. My wife Glenda and I have been talking about where we want to take our kids for vacation. One option is the mountains, which are scenic and pleasant. Another is the beach, which is fun, too. It's important to take plenty of sunscreen when heading there, or you're sure to return home with at least one souvenir—a sunburn! On summer days by the sea, the temperature goes from hot to hotter to hotter still.

That's somewhat the way it is when our priorities lead us toward the lions' den. As we consistently model Daniel's three-fold commitment to holiness, truth and a transformed (instead of a conformed) lifestyle, opposition tends to increase by degrees. First, we find that some people don't like what they see in us. Then, they begin to *say* that they don't like it. Finally, they start *showing* that they don't like it. As a result of this resentment, we can find ourselves in some pretty tight spots.

I don't know how big the lions' den was, but I'm sure Daniel would have welcomed a much larger room when he checked in and found that he had been assigned multiple occupancy!

To avoid being surprised by our own encounter with the lions' den, it's helpful to look at how and why opposition can mount in response to a distinctive lifestyle. By being aware, we will be better prepared to deal with the challenges which confront us when we do end up facing those ferocious fur coats.

As we noted before, Daniel chapter six makes clear that the aging prophet was quite a hit in the court of Darius.

> *. . . Daniel began distinguishing himself . . .*
> (verse 3).

This was the product of his life-long pattern of integrity. The very reason Darius had put Daniel and two other commissioners over the affairs of his kingdom was that "the king might not suffer loss" (verse 2). The king's net worth flourished under Daniel—so much so, that Darius intended to make Daniel second-in-command to himself. The result: the other commissioners and satraps didn't like it. Daniel's excellence provoked their jealousy and hatred.

Then, they began to *say* they didn't like it, talking with one another about this troublesome man. It's easy to imagine how their conversations must have gone:

"He's making us all look bad."

"Why does he think his way is so much better than ours?"

"Why does he have to be so honest?"

"Why can't he just go with the flow?"

"We've got to stop him now before he gains any more power."

Their murmuring in the hallways of the palace developed into a full-scale movement of opposition. They began to wonder how they might undo this consistently truthful man. The only problem was, "they could find no ground of accusation or evidence of corruption, inasmuch as he was faithful . . ." (verse 4).

Finally, they hatched their plot to make his devotion to the Lord the very thing which brought him down. When someone suffers for his or her commitment to God, that's called persecution.

If the truth were known, most Christians probably wish the word "persecution" weren't in the Bible. It is, though—over 70 times in one form or another. When we dedicate our lives to pleasing God and doing His will, we should not be surprised when persecution leaps off the pages of Scripture and breathes in our faces.

Paul told Timothy, "And indeed, all who desire to live godly in Christ Jesus will be persecuted" (2 Timothy 3:12).

How could Paul make such a guarantee? Because of the truth he declared to the Christians at Ephesus:

> *For our struggle is not against flesh and blood, but against the rulers, against the powers, against the world forces of this darkness, against the spiritual forces of wickedness in the heavenly places* (Ephesians 6:12).

Paul knew that believers in Jesus Christ are involved in a war which has been raging since before the Garden of Eden. This spiritual battle is the result of Satan's rebellion against God and his subsequent efforts to thwart His purposes and destroy His Kingdom.

Satan was originally an angelic being, created by God to carry out His bidding. Psalm 103:20-21 gives the angelic job description:

> *Bless the Lord, you His angels,*
> *Mighty in strength, who perform His word,*
> *Obeying the voice of His word!*
> *Bless the Lord, all you His hosts,*
> *You who serve Him, doing His will.*

Satan, also known as Lucifer (Isaiah 14:12, KJV), was apparently a cherub charged with the responsibility of guarding God's throne (Ezekiel 28:14). Not content with this position of prominence, he sought to usurp God's authority, or in other words, to stage a palace coup.

> *. . . I will make myself like the Most High, he declared* (Isaiah 14:14).

Satan was joined in his rebellion by other wayward angels. God expelled Satan and his cohorts from heaven to await their final judgement and condemnation (Luke 10:18; Matthew 25:41). Till that time, God is allowing these evil beings to operate on earth and to seek our allegiance in their struggle against Him.

So what does this have to do with Daniel? Well, Satan was the architect of the lions' den; his paw prints were all over it. In the New Testament, he is referred to as a "roaring lion seeking someone to devour" (1 Peter 5:8). He wanted Daniel for dinner.

Fortunately, Daniel was "tough stuff," spiritually speaking. As we'll see later, the devil had to order another dish. But, do you know what? Despite Daniel's deliverance, the devil dines well.

Where Can I Get Something To Eat?

One of the questions I ask when I check into a hotel is, "Where can I get something to eat?" Some of the restaurants I've patronized offered truly fine dining. Others I would prefer to forget. Either the food was poorly prepared, the service was slack, or the company was unpleasant. Whom we eat with is often as important as where we eat.

May I be honest with you?

When it comes to "spiritual dining," every human being from Adam and Eve onward has chosen to dine with the devil. Not one of us has opted to sit at God's table, every meal, all the time. Each of us has, in our own way, rebelled against God; as Satan did, we have sought to be like Him . . . without Him.

The Bible teaches this sad truth:

> *There is none righteous, not even one;*
> *There is none who understands,*
> *There is none who seeks for God;*
> *All have turned aside, together they have become*
> *useless;*
> *There is none who does good,*
> *There is not even one* (Romans 3:10-12).

Every one of us has at one time or another opted to live our own stubborn, prideful way rather than obeying God. As proof, consider the Ten Commandments (Exodus 20:1-17). None of us has always kept every one of God's commands. James, the half-brother of our Lord, declared:

> *For whoever keeps the whole law and yet stumbles in one point, he has become guilty of all. For He who said, "Do not commit adultery," also said, "Do not commit murder." Now if you do not commit adultery, but do commit murder, you have become a transgressor of the law* (James 2:10-11).

Jesus made clear in the Sermon on the Mount (Matthew 5-7) that cherishing evil thoughts in our hearts is sin, just as much as expressing them outwardly. Against God's perfect standard, then, none of us can say that we are innocent.

Romans 3:23 sums it up:

> *. . . for all have sinned and fall short of the glory of God . . .*

In choosing to sin against God, each of us has sided with Satan and deserves the fate awaiting him—eternal condemnation and punishment.

> *For the wages of sin is death . . .* (Romans 6:23a).

The wonderful message of the Gospel, though, is this:

> *. . . but the free gift of God is eternal life in Christ Jesus our Lord* (Romans 6:23b).

God offers us this alternative because He loves us:

> *But God demonstrates His own love toward us, in that while we were yet sinners, Christ died for us* (Romans 5:8).

All we need to do to be forgiven for our sins and restored to a right relationship with God is to trust in Christ as the basis of our acceptance before God:

> *For God so loved the world, that He gave His only begotten Son, that whoever believes in Him should not perish, but have eternal life* (John 3:16).

God's gracious offer of pardon and salvation requires a response from us. Jesus called all who heard Him to "repent and believe the Gospel" (Mark 1:15).

A friend of mine who teaches a seventh-grade Sunday school class always makes this point by setting a box of doughnuts on the floor in the middle of the room. In order to enjoy the doughnuts (I like 'em hot), each student has to take one for himself or herself. Otherwise, the doughnuts remain simply a gift that has been offered, but not received and enjoyed. That's the way it is with the Good News about Christ.

> *But as many as received Him, to them He gave the right to become children of God, even to those who believe in His name . . .* (John 1:12).

> *. . . if you confess with your mouth Jesus as Lord, and believe in your heart that God raised Him from the dead, you shall be saved; for with the heart man believes, resulting in righteousness, and with the mouth he confesses, resulting in salvation* (Romans 10:9-10).

When you and I believe the Biblical message about Christ and begin to base our lives on a relationship with Him, a wonderful thing happens: He becomes our dinner partner!

Jesus Himself said in Revelation 3:20:

> Behold, I stand at the door and knock; if anyone hears My voice and opens the door, I will come in to him and will dine with him, and he with Me.

Think of it—the Lord Jesus Christ Himself wants to keep company with you and me! If the President of the United States or some other respected world leader invited us to a meal, we would go to great lengths to attend. The message of the Gospel is that God's Son wants to relate personally and intimately with each of us, both in this life and for all eternity. All we have to do to get in on the experience is accept His invitation.

Have you ever said "yes" to Christ? If not, you can do it right now, right where you are. Simply put this book down and express to God your desire to quit living your own way, to quit dining with the devil.

Tell Him you believe that Jesus Christ is the way He has provided for you to be forgiven for your sins, and that you want Christ's death on the cross to count on your behalf, as the punishment you deserve but which He took in your place.

Ask Christ to come and live in you by His Spirit, and to make you a new person, one whose life is transformed by the presence of Jesus Himself.

Have you done it?

Congratulations! You have become connected to the only One in all of heaven, earth and hell who can make your life as full and purposeful as it was meant to be.

You have become related to the One who supremely satisfies the needs of the human heart.

> *Jesus said to them, "I am the bread of life; he who comes to Me shall not hunger, and he who believes in Me shall never thirst"* (John 6:35).

> *". . . whoever drinks of the water that I shall give him shall never thirst; but the water that I shall give him shall become in him a well of water springing up to eternal life"* (John 4:14).

By placing your faith in Jesus Christ, you have become a child of God. As you live in fellowship with Him day by day, He will strengthen you to live a life which is holy and true, and which conforms not to the world but to His perfect nature.

Now, wherever you go, your Lord and Savior Jesus Christ will be with you, even when your path leads you where Daniel's did—into the lions' den.

What's The Charge?

Years ago, a television series featured an immigrant who came to America with no money and no place to stay. A funny thing happened, though—someone mistook him for a rich international dignitary, and he was warmly invited by the management of a fine hotel to check in there. Believing him to be wealthy, the hotel did not require him to establish his credit; they told him just to charge his expenses by signing his name to his bills.

The immigrant did not understand this system of doing business, and thought he was being given free lodging. He lived quite well and enjoyed it immensely. *What a great country America is*, he thought. *Where else could a poor immigrant come and live like royalty?* Then, the time came to settle his bill.

Much to his chagrin (and that of the hotel management), he discovered he had been accruing charges—heavy charges—which he could not pay. This American fairy tale lost its luster when he was forced to retire his debt by working for the hotel as a bellhop.

Fortunately for the hapless immigrant, this was

just a television series; I don't remember that it lasted very long. For Christians committed as Daniel was to holiness, truth and a transformed lifestyle, however, the experience of having charges—accusations—leveled against them can be all too real. In fact, the road to the lions' den is paved with unfair accusations.

The reason for this is simple. Satan, who is the ultimate enemy of holiness, truth and every other attribute of God, is by nature an accuser. The Bible calls him "the accuser of our brethren" (Revelation 12:10). One of the clearest demonstrations of this fact is found in the Old Testament book of Job. In Job chapter one, Satan took a break from the activity in which he is involved even to this day—"roaming about on the earth and walking around on it" (verse 7)—and appeared before God. God pointed out to him the distinctive lifestyle of Job:

> *Have you considered my servant Job? For there is no one like him on the earth, a blameless and upright man, fearing God and turning away from evil* (verse 8).

Then Satan began to accuse Job:

> *Does Job fear God for nothing? Hast Thou not made a hedge about him and his house and all that he has, on every side? Thou hast blessed the work of his hands, and his possessions have increased in the land. But put forth Thy hand now and touch all that he has; he will surely curse Thee to Thy face* (verses 10-11).

The book then goes on to describe the suffering God allowed Satan to inflict on Job; Satan's further accusations against Job when Job refused to curse God; and the abundant blessings God eventually bestowed on Job in response to his faith and perseverance. Job emerged from his trial "as gold" (Job 23:10); Satan, as the frustrated accuser.

To this moment, however, he continues his vicious work:

- leveling charges against believers, before God;

- leveling charges against God, before believers; and

- leveling charges against believers, before other believers.

I'm not too concerned with what Satan tells the Lord about me. God knows my heart better than I do, and His Son Jesus Christ is my Defender before Him.

> *My little children, I am writing these things to you that you may not sin. And if anyone sins, we have an Advocate with the Father, Jesus Christ the righteous . . .* (1 John 2:1).

We should be deeply concerned, though, over what Satan tries to tell us about God, and what he tries to tell us believers about one another.

Our parents Adam and Eve got into trouble in the Garden of Eden because they listened when Satan, in the form of the serpent, impugned God's motives:

> *Indeed, has God said, "You shall not eat from any tree of the garden"?* (Genesis 3:1).

God had not said that, but Satan was baiting Eve by suggesting to her lies about God. She said it was the

tree in the middle of the Garden—the tree of the knowledge of good and evil—from which they were not to eat,
under penalty of death.

> *And the serpent said to the woman, "You surely
> shall not die! For God knows that in the day you eat
> from it your eyes will be opened, and you will be like
> God, knowing good and evil"* (Genesis 3:4-5).

What Satan was insinuating was that God wanted
to "cheat" Adam and Eve out of something good. How
many people have bought that lie today! The truth is
set forth, though, in Psalm 84:11:

> *For the Lord God is a sun and shield;*
> *The Lord gives grace and glory;*
> *No good thing does He withhold from those who*
> *walk uprightly.*

Satan wants you and me to think (1) that God is
unconcerned about us and does not really love us, (2)
that He is intent on making our lives miserable, and
(3) that He is not trustworthy. How those same thoughts
must have gnawed at Daniel that night in the lions'
den!

Perhaps they are gnawing at you right now. If so,
reject them. They are lies being pressed upon you by
Satan, the enemy of your soul. He wants you to believe
that he offers the best alternative for your life. To be
sure, he can be quite convincing. The Bible warns
twice, however, that "there is a way which seems right
to a man, but its end is the way of death" (Proverbs
14:12; 16:25).

Satan also attempts to destroy relationships between

believers by planting in our minds evil thoughts about
one another. He thrives on stirring up discord, mis-
trust, anger and hatred. He knows that if he can get us
fighting each other, we won't be effective witnesses in
the world around us. I believe that's why the Lord
Jesus prayed in John 17:20-21:

> *I do not ask in behalf of these alone, but for those*
> *also who believe in Me through their word;* that
> they may all be one; *even as Thou, Father, art in*
> *Me, and I in Thee, that they also may be in Us;* that
> the world may believe that Thou didst send Me.

Maybe one of your relationships, or perhaps even
your local church, has been torn apart by misunder-
standing and accusation. While these things are in-
cited by Satan, we are responsible for participating in
them. We are not just helpless victims; we can choose
not to take part.

A game I've seen kids play in hotel swimming pools
is "sharks and minnows." Some choose to be minnows;
others choose to be sharks; the sharks then try to
capture the minnows, while the minnows try to escape.

In the Body of Christ, most of us have chosen at one
time or another to be "sharks" and have gone after
"minnows"—our innocent brothers and sisters—with a
passion. In some churches, the game has led to a feed-
ing frenzy.

My friend, the game has gone too far. It's time to put
a stop to it. Our enemy loves to watch it happen . . . just
as Daniel's foes savored the prospect of his being
devoured by the lions.

Is This It?
(Part One)

A pastor I know was attending a Christian conference with his wife, and they were staying in a hotel run by the conference center. If you've taken part in similar events, you know how friendly the participants can become in a short period of time. Before long, people are visiting from room to room, swapping stories like old pals, keeping an eye on each other's kids, and even leaving their doors unlocked.

This was the case at my friend's conference—and it nearly led to his divorce! It seems my friend's wife left their room for awhile. When she returned, she walked through the door to see a pair of feet she recognized as her husband's sticking out from under the sheets ... and another woman in the same bed.

My friend's wife had been enjoying the close fellowship between conference participants, but this was carrying things too far!

"Get out of that bed!" she shrieked.

To her surprise, the startled male who looked up was not her husband. In fact, the clothes, suitcases and other items in the room were not hers either—she had entered the wrong room! All the doors looked alike and she hadn't checked the numbers carefully enough. Did she beat a hasty retreat!

When staying in a hotel, it is helpful to ask yourself, *before* entering what appears to be your room, "Is this it?" That's also a timely question to ask when you think you may be about to check into your own personal lions' den.

Perhaps the best way to recognize a lions' den in our lives is to reflect on the characteristics which marked the one Daniel encountered, then be on the alert for those same factors in our circumstances.

First of all, let's address what a lions' den is *not*. Not every difficult experience we have is truly a lions' den. We must avoid the temptation to consider ourselves martyrs when, actually, we are suffering for reasons besides our distinctive lifestyle.

Daniel did not end up in the lions' den because of his personal negligence. He did not go about his duties in Darius' court in a sloppy, haphazard way.

> *. . . Daniel began distinguishing himself . . . they could find no ground of accusation . . . no negligence . . . was to be found in him* (Daniel 6:3,4).

Daniel did not end up in the lions' den because he was corrupt, either.

> *. . . they could find no . . . evidence of corruption . . . no negligence or corruption was to be found in him.*

These amazing statements could be made about Daniel because, in the words of the same verse, "he was faithful."

Ah, faithfulness ... sometimes it seems like an endangered species!

Think about the day in which we live: faithfulness is often the exception rather than the rule.

Employees cheat their bosses; bosses cheat their company shareholders; shareholders cheat the government.

Politicians cheat on the men and women who elect them to office. Men and women—spouses—cheat on each other.

Kids cheat in school, and even teachers cheat in administering achievement tests to their students, so that their classes will score higher and they will look like better teachers!

One of my favorite contemporary Christian songs goes by a title which must have been Daniel's prayer, and which desperately needs to be ours: "Find Us Faithful."

The Lord Jesus Himself called for faithfulness among Christians in the period between His first and second coming:

> *Who then is the faithful and sensible slave whom his master put in charge of his household to give them their food at the proper time? Blessed is that slave whom his master finds so doing when he comes* (Matthew 25:45-46).

Faithfulness is an attribute of God Himself and a trait He looks for in His people. It is to be the rule and not the exception, for it is the fruit or result of the Holy Spirit's presence and work in an individual's life.

But the fruit of the Spirit is . . . faithfulness . . .
(Galatians 5:22).

Do you have any fruit in your life right now? Does faithfulness characterize you, even in seemingly "small" matters?

Jesus said, "He who is faithful in a very little thing is faithful also in much; and he who is unrighteous in a very little thing is unrighteous also in much" (Luke 16:10).

If you're like me, you're probably feeling twinges of guilt as you read our Lord's words and consider your own life. Too often, I'm not faithful in "little" things—but I want to be. We can find comfort in the fact that God is merciful and compassionate, and that in the Person of the Holy Spirit, He comes alongside all who trust in Him to bring about faithfulness in our lives.

. . . for it is God who is at work in you, both to will and to work for His good pleasure (Philippians 4:13).

Daniel was faithful, and we can be too. The secret is in asking God to take our natural inclinations toward corruption and negligence out of our hearts.

. . . no negligence or corruption was to be found in him.

Jesus taught that evil in our lives issues from our hearts (Mark 7:21-23). Our hearts are the wellspring of our lives, and we are to guard them carefully (Proverbs 4:23).

Christ spelled out the blessing connected with doing so in His Sermon on the Mount:

Blessed are the pure in heart, for they shall see God (Matthew 5:8).

Daniel was a man accustomed to seeing the living God do amazing things in his life—at least in part, because he was faithful. His stay in the lions' den was not the result of negligence or corruption; neither are our personal visits there.

Nor was Daniel's trip to the lions' den the result of foolish provocation. In other words, Daniel didn't go looking for trouble. Even though he was a man of godly conviction, it wasn't his style to pick a fight. Rather, he went out of his way to avoid one at times. This was shown by the manner in which he handled that first crisis early in his captivity, the one related to eating King Nebuchadnezzar's food. In that instance, he exercised great discretion and practiced skillful diplomacy in working toward the end he desired.

. . . he sought permission from the commander of the officials that he might not defile himself (Daniel 1:8).

God worked on Daniel's behalf by granting him "favor and compassion in the sight of the commander of the officials" (Daniel 1:9). The commander wanted to grant Daniel's request but was fearful of losing his own head if he went against the king's wishes, so Daniel lobbied the overseer who had immediate responsibility for serving the captives' food. He proposed a specific plan:

Please test your servants for ten days, and let us be given some vegetables to eat and water to drink.

Then let our appearance be observed in your pres-
ence, and the appearance of the youths who are
eating the king's choice food; and deal with your
servants according to what you see
(Daniel 1:12-13).

God blessed Daniel's approach, causing the overseer to listen to him. How different the outcome might
have been if Daniel had pitched a fit and unnecessarily
provoked his captors; he surely would have been "force
fed" or killed, or both!

Daniel, however, was "endowed with understand-
ing, and discerning knowledge" (Daniel 1:4).

And as for every matter of wisdom and understand-
ing about which the king consulted them [Daniel
and his friends, Shadrach, Meshach and Abednego],
he found them ten times better than all the magi-
cians and conjurers who were in all his realm
(Daniel 1:20).

The lions' den was not the result of indiscretion on
his part, nor is it for us. To be sure, when we foolishly
provoke a conflict, or when we prove to be negligent or
corrupt, we do often suffer. Such suffering, however,
should be viewed as justly deserved, as the conse-
quence of our wrong actions, and not as "suffering for
Jesus."

The Apostle Peter pointed this out to early Christians who were undergoing persecution for living faithfully in a pagan, hostile society:

For this finds favor, if for the sake of conscience
toward God a man bears up under sorrows when
suffering unjustly. For what credit is there if, when
you sin and are harshly treated, you endure it with

patience? But if when you do what is right and suffer
for it you patiently endure it, this finds favor with
God. For you have been called for this purpose, since
Christ also suffered for you, leaving you an example
for you to follow in His steps, who committed no sin,
nor was any deceit found in His mouth; and while
being reviled, He did not revile in return; while suf-
fering, He uttered no threats, but kept entrusting
Himself to Him who judges righteously . . .
(1 Peter 2:19-23).

Peter made his point even clearer by saying:

By no means let any of you suffer as a murderer, or
thief, or evildoer, or a troublesome meddler; but if
anyone suffers as a Christian, let him not feel ashamed,
but in that name let him glorify God . . . let those also
who suffer according to the will of God entrust their
souls to a faithful Creator in doing what is right (1
Peter 4:15-16, 19).

Persecution does come to those who live distinctively. As we've said before, it's guaranteed. Our responsibility is to make sure that, when we suffer, we do so
for the right reasons. Then, when that's the case, we
can actually have joy in our hearts as we check into our
own personal lions' den. In the words of Peter:

Beloved, do not be surprised at the fiery ordeal among
you, which comes upon you for your testing, as though
some strange thing were happening to you; but to the
degree that you share the sufferings of Christ, keep
on rejoicing; so that also at the revelation of His
glory, you may rejoice with exultation. If you are
reviled for the name of Christ, you are blessed, be-
cause the Spirit of glory and of God rests upon you (1
Peter 4:12-14).

Is This It?
(Part Two)

Daniel's stay in the lions' den wasn't the result of negligence, corruption or foolish provocation on his part, and our personal lions' dens aren't, either.

"What, then, *is* a lions' den?" you may ask. "How am I to know when I check into one myself?"

For Daniel, the lions' den was a literal place filled with literal lions with literally sharp teeth. Few of us will find ourselves in such a spot; his lions' den, though, had five characteristics which we can expect to encounter as we live distinctively:

1. It was a difficult situation he found himself in expressly because of his allegiance to God.

2. It was the result of choosing to please God rather than people.

3. It arose in the course of daily duty.

4. It was forced upon him by circumstances he did not seek but could not, with integrity, avoid.

5. It posed a serious threat; the stakes were high, either way he chose to act.

Let's look at these characteristics one by one so that

we will recognize a lions' den when we see it before us.

1. It was a difficult situation he found himself in expressly because of his allegiance to God.

Plain and simple, Daniel's commitment to the Lord was what got him into trouble. Not even his enemies could bring any other charge against him which would stick. That's the way it was with Christ, too: not even those who opposed Him could legitimately accuse Him of any wrongdoing. They just didn't like that fact that He was (and is) God.

When we find ourselves in a difficult situation because we are dedicated to Christ, that's one indication that we may have arrived—in the lions' den!

The early church leader Stephen experienced this for himself. Stephen was a man like Daniel, "of good reputation, full of the Spirit and of wisdom" (Acts 6:3). He was "full of faith and of the Holy Spirit" (Acts 6:5). He was "full of grace and power" (Acts 6:8). He also caught a rock in the head for his faithful witness to Jesus Christ (Acts 7:58)!

Stephen was the early church's first martyr, expressly because of his allegiance to God. The other characteristics of Daniel's lions' den were also true of Stephen's situation. If Daniel had been able to choose a roommate, Stephen would have been great company.

How about you? Have you found yourself in a difficult situation because of your allegiance to God? In your job or, if you're a student, at school, has being committed to Christ placed you in a tight spot? If so, take heart; Daniel, Stephen and other faithful men and women throughout history have landed in the same place. You're not the first believer (and you won't be the last) whom our adversary Satan—that hungry, roaring lion —has sought to devour.

> *But resist him, firm in your faith, knowing that the same experiences of suffering are being accomplished by your brethren who are in the world. And after you have suffered for a little while, the God of all grace, who called you to His eternal glory in Christ, will Himself perfect, confirm, strengthen and establish you* (1 Peter 5:9-10).

2. It was the result of choosing to please God rather than people.

Daniel did not have to go to the lions' den; he did have a choice. He could have quit praying to Almighty God—just for 30 days (Daniel 6:7)—and everything would have been all right.

At least, that's what Daniel's enemies wanted him to believe. Had he compromised, however, his testimony for God would have been undermined. Daniel didn't have to go to the lions' den—but he did have to make a decision. Would he please the people around him, or would he please God?

It's important to notice that Daniel's enemies did not ask Darius to outlaw prayer to the one true God permanently. Rather, they got him to ban it temporarily, only for a month. Much of the evil in our society today slips in the door "temporarily."

"Just permit this or prohibit that for the time being,"

the reasoning often goes. "Then we'll take a look at the situation and, if necessary, change things back the way they were."

Too often, though, the "temporary" becomes permanent. We as Christians ought to be alert to efforts in our government, and even in our churches and denominations, to enact "temporary" measures which dishonor God, deny Christian values, and conflict with the Bible. We should be swift in becoming well-informed about the issues in question, and in responding with both love and courage. When we are not, then—before we know it—permanent damage can occur.

Daniel could have avoided the lions' den, if he had just been willing to please people rather than God. But he wasn't ... so he didn't. What a contrast he was to the religious leaders of Jesus' day. Of them the Apostle John wrote:

> *Nevertheless many even of the rulers believed in*
> *Him, but because of the Pharisees they were not*
> *confessing Him, lest they should be put out of the*
> *synagogue; for they loved the approval of men rather*
> *than the approval of God* (John 12:42-43).

You and I should pray that John's haunting indictment won't be true of us. Even if our tendency is to cave in to peer pressure rather than resist evil for Christ's sake, we can become strong by the power of the Holy Spirit. Jesus' first disciples deserted him when He was arrested; under the Spirit's control, though, they eventually became quite bold—so much so that, when they were arrested and threatened for their witness, their reply was:

> *We must obey God rather than men* (Acts 5:29).

When push comes to shove and we side with God . . . only to find ourselves eyeball to eyeball with a bunch of drooling beasts . . . it's a safe bet we're entering our own personal lions' den.

3. It arose in the course of daily duty.

"There I was, minding my own business, when suddenly . . ."

Daniel could have made a statement like that about how he ended up in the lions' den. Our own encounters with the lions generally arise in the same manner.

Isn't it amazing how quickly our daily routines as believers can become fierce struggles—if not for our lives, at least for our spiritual integrity? This has always been the case. Consider the following:

- A handsome Hebrew slave in Egypt is tending to his master's affairs, when his master's wife tries to entice him into an affair with her. He resists, even running from the house to escape—only to end up in prison. Thus, Joseph was welcomed to the lions' den (see Genesis 39).

- A young Jewish shepherd is instructed by his father to take some food to his brothers, who are serving in Israel's army. As he arrives, he finds a fierce, pagan warrior taunting the troops, who are paralyzed with fear. Loyal to his king and jealous for the glory of his God, the shepherd takes on the giant, defeats him, and becomes a hero—only to have the king he fought for turn against him and try to kill him, forcing him into hiding. That was David's introduction to the lions' den (see 1 Samuel 17-19).

- A small group of Christians is on the way to prayer meeting when they meet a slave-girl who is demon-possessed. One of them commands the demon to leave her in the Name of Jesus Christ and the girl is wondrously set free. Her masters, however, are less than happy because they have been exploiting the girl's condition for their personal profit. They seize two of the believers and have them beaten with rods, thrown into prison, and placed in stocks. That's how Paul and Silas checked into the lions' den (see Acts 16).

Lions' dens arise in the course of daily duty. They just happen as we go about our business with the Lord. That's partly why the Scriptures warn us to "be on the alert." Lions' dens are seldom like holidays on a calendar for which we can make special plans and preparations.

4. It was forced upon him by circumstances he did not seek but could not, with integrity, avoid.

As we pointed out earlier, Daniel did not foolishly provoke the conflict in which he found himself. Rather, it was forced upon him by his evil enemies; once that occurred, however, he could not in good conscience avoid making a stand.

Both the Bible and history are filled with examples of people who have been forced to make a stand for God and His Kingdom or lose their spiritual edge. In response to the idolatry of his day, aged Joshua challenged the people of Israel to "choose for yourselves today whom you will serve" (Joshua 24:15).

Daniel's friends Shadrach, Meshach and Abednego had to make that choice when Nebuchadnezzar commanded them to bow down or be burned (see Daniel 3). Jesus said,

> *"Render to Caesar the things that are Caesar's, and to God the things that are God's"* (Mark 12:17).

Like it or not, you and I must sometimes cast our ballots in contests we cannot in good conscience avoid. Often, there really isn't any neutral ground. To look the other way is to vote . . . against God.

What issues have been forced upon you from which you cannot turn away and still preserve your testimony for Christ, as well as your self-respect? Where are you being compelled to make a stand which will alienate some people and, quite possibly, pit you against even your closest friends, all for the sake of Christ?

Wherever that is for you, my friend, take note: it's the door to your own lions' den.

5. It posed a serious threat; the stakes were high, either way he chose to act.

Some things in life are worth fighting over; others are not. Daniel was wise enough to know the difference. For example:

- Daniel's native language was Hebrew; Nebuchadnezzar ordered that he be taught Chaldean (Daniel 1:4). Apparently, he proved to be quite a good student.

- Daniel was a Hebrew name; the Hebrew names of his three friends were Hananiah, Mishael, and Azariah. In Babylon, they were given the names Belteshazzar, Shadrach, Meshach and Abednego (Daniel 1:7). They all answered to their new names.

The picture which emerges is that Daniel understood the importance of contesting the vital issues. In other matters, he humbly submitted to authority and gave preference to the wishes of others.

Let me be blunt here: being wholeheartedly committed to Christ, whose cross is an "offense" to the world (1 Peter 2:8), does not mean that we have to be offensive people. Yet how often that's the case!

Some Christians appear to believe that living distinctively means bristling at every idea they don't agree with. My friend, let's call that practice what it is—stubborn, selfish pride. Much damage has been done by such conduct. Churches have been torn apart and outsiders repulsed—all because, in the name of conviction, believers have been abrasive.

It's time to strip off the spiritual cloak in which we hide such behavior and force it to stand naked—and judged—in the light of God's Word:

> *Do nothing from selfishness or empty conceit, but with humility of mind let each of you regard one*

another as more important than himself; do not merely
look out for your own personal interests, but also for
the interests of others. Have this attitude in your-
selves which was also in Christ Jesus, who, although
He existed in the form of God, did not regard equality
with God a thing to be grasped, but emptied Himself,
taking the form of a bondservant . . .
(Philippians 2:5-7).

Some matters in which we do not see eye to eye with others simply are not worth fighting about. This is true in the Body of Christ, and it's also true in relation to the world. Jesus Himself showed that He was concerned about unnecessarily offending unbelievers when it came to paying tax for support of the Temple.

Among first-century Jews, the practice was to collect the equivalent of about 32 cents per person for use in maintaining the Temple. One day some Jews asked Peter whether Jesus paid the tax, and Peter said that He did. Afterwards, as Peter and Jesus discussed the matter, Jesus made clear that He, the Son of God, was not obligated to pay for the support of the Temple.

"But," He said to Peter, "lest we give them offense, go
to the sea, and throw in a hook, and take the first fish
that comes up; and when you open its mouth, you will
find a stater [a coin worth about 64 cents, enough to
pay the tax for both of them]. *Take that and give it to*
them for you and Me" (Matthew 17:27).

Think of it—to avoid offending others over a 32-cent issue, Jesus performed a miracle! Yet how often we raise our hackles and get into fights over such matters.

Daniel chose to contest issues which really mattered, and we should follow his example. The stakes were indeed high in Daniel chapter six. On the one hand, submitting to the king's decree would make him an idolater; on the other hand, refusing would, as far as he knew, cost him his life—so he made his stand.

True lions' dens in our lives are not the result of petty squabbles over insignificant questions. They are the result of standing for God in matters of importance and in which the consequences for us are sure to be great, either way we choose to act.

As Daniel was escorted to the lions' den, he must have felt a great sense of satisfaction that he wasn't about to die for something so trivial as, say, arguing over the color of carpet in the king's palace (or a house of worship!). He was going there for something that counted from the viewpoint of heaven.

Enjoy Your Stay

For children on vacation, getting there—wherever "there" might be—sometimes seems to take a lifetime. Stops to fuel the car, check directions, eat, visit the restroom, and look at souvenirs can make a kid think that vacation consists of riding in the car for many hours, and that no destination exists. Sooner or later, though, the family does arrive; then, the agenda shifts from "getting there" to "enjoying it." That's the way it works in God's family with the lions' den, too.

Maybe by now you've identified a situation or two in your own life fitting the description of a lions' den. You may even be in the midst of one right now. Once we do arrive there, the question becomes, how do we "enjoy" it—or perhaps more accurately, how can we survive and emerge victorious? Again, we can learn a lot from our friend Daniel.

In chapter 11 of the New Testament Book of Hebrews, we are given a clue as to what went on in the lions' den the night Daniel stayed there. Hebrews 11 is often referred to as "faith's hall of fame," because it defines faith and describes how it enabled a variety of individuals in Scripture to face the challenges confronting them. The chapter begins:

> *Now faith is the assurance of things hoped for, the conviction of things not seen. For by it the men of old gained approval* (Hebrews 11:1-2).

Then, in verses 32 and 33, we get our clue:

> *And what more shall I say? For time will fail me if I tell of Gideon, Barak, Samson, Jephthah, of David and Samuel and the prophets, who by faith conquered kingdoms, performed acts of righteousness, obtained promises, shut the mouths of lions . . .*

Did you catch that last one? ". . . shut the mouths of lions . . ."

According to the passage, once Daniel checked into the lions' den, he kept himself from being the entree of the day "by faith."

Maybe you wonder how that worked. "Faith" may sound a little abstract in the face of real, live, hungry lions. There's more in the word "faith," though, than we may realize.

Faith carries the meaning of "clinging to, adhering to, relying upon." Hebrews 11 begins by saying it "is the assurance of things hoped for, the conviction of things not seen."

It's helpful to know that literal lions—the kind you can see in Africa—feed themselves by watching a herd of gazelle or some other species, then picking out a weak straggler and pouncing on it. Lions are masters at detecting weakness in their prey and, when they spot it, they go after it with gusto. Satan works like that.

The lions Daniel faced that night must not have sensed any weakness in him. How could that be? Daniel was clinging to, adhering to, relying upon God. Though he could not see God, he was convinced that God was with him. This gave him assurance and hope, even when faced by man-eating lions.

As Proverbs 28:1 says:

> *The wicked flee when no one is pursuing,*
> *But the righteous are bold as a lion.*

In short, Daniel's survival in the lions' den was at least partially due to his confidence in God's presence, power and love; this gave him a strength of spirit that even the lions could sense. The same was true of the Lord Jesus in the days of His flesh, of whom the Scripture says:

> *And He was in the wilderness forty days being*
> *tempted by Satan; and he was with the wild*
> *beasts . . .* (Mark 1:13).

We'll see later that Daniel also attributed his deliverance to an angel sent by God to shut the lions' mouths. The important point is that Daniel was not depending on himself. He was totally yielded to God and His will for his life. If God did not help him, he would die, and He was prepared to accept death as the price of faithfulness.

Daniel had no guarantee that he would emerge from the lions' den unscathed. His attitude must have been the same as his friends—Shadrach, Meshach and Abednego—when they were about to be thrown into the fiery furnace:

. . . our God whom we serve is able to deliver us
from the furnace of blazing fire; and He will deliver
us out of your hand, O king. But even if He does not,
let it be known to you, O king, that we are not going
to serve your gods or worship the golden image that
you have set up (Daniel 3:17-18).

Suffering Job demonstrated the same attitude when he declared, "Though He [God] slay me, I will hope in Him" (Job 13:15).

Daniel too must have determined that whatever God allowed to happen, he would accept. The fact that he could feel that way in the face of personal peril was in itself a miracle! The second miracle occurred when God, by his angel, caused the lions to wait for another selection from the menu.

What does all of this say to you and me? That faith is the key to surviving and even thriving in our own personal lions' dens. Clinging to, adhering to, relying upon God . . . trusting in His presence, power and love . . . is our ticket to triumph. That's why the risen Lord Jesus told His disciples:

All authority has been given to Me in heaven and on
earth [His power]. *Go therefore and make disciples*
of all the nations . . . and lo, I am with you always,
even to the end of the age [His presence] (Matthew 28:18-20).

Having faith in the midst of our lions' dens does not necessarily mean that we will emerge, as Daniel did, untouched. Hebrews 11 also lists other heroes of faith who

were tortured . . . experienced mockings and

> *scourgings, yes, also chains and imprisonment.*
> *They were stoned, they were sawn in two, they were*
> *tempted, they were put to death with the sword; they*
> *went about in sheepskins, in goatskins, being desti-*
> *tute, afflicted, ill-treated . . .* (verses 35-37).

Bad things do happen to godly people through no sin or error of their own. Some emerge from the lions' den with all their limbs intact; others graduate through the lions' den to heaven—the very dwelling place of God. Either outcome is brought about by faith, and both outcomes are miracles for which we should give God glory.

The alternative is "faith failure," which leads not to deliverance or promotion, but denial of God, compromise with the world, and surrender to Satan. Thus, when we face the lions, it's time to pray for our own miracle!

The mention of prayer raises the question: what was Daniel praying for after he knew the decree had been signed making prayer to God a capital offense?

He may have been reflecting on that beloved psalm penned by his ancestor King David:

> *The Lord is my shepherd . . .*
> *Even though I walk through the valley of the*
> *shadow of death,*
> *I fear no evil; for Thou art with me . . .*
> (Psalm 23:1,4).

We're not told precisely what words he used in this instance. However, in chapter nine of the Book of Daniel, one of Daniel's prayers is recorded word for word. There, he confessed the sin of his people and claimed

God's promise to deliver them from bondage and return them to their land. God answered this prayer by sending His people back to Jerusalem under King Cyrus.

What that tells us is that Daniel knew how to pray humbly and contritely, in a way which pleased the Father. So did Christ. When He prayed in Gethsemane on the eve of His crucifixion, He said:

> *My Father, if this cannot pass away unless I drink it, Thy will be done* (Matthew 26:42).

As Daniel faced the prospect of suffering, he must have been praying like Jesus—asking for wisdom . . . pleading that his faith, his reliance upon God, would not fail. He was probably also praying for those who hated him. That's a good example for us to follow as we check into the lions' den.

House Rules

Most hotels are required by law to post in their rooms a list of rules guests are to follow. Often, the list is attached to the back side of the door and gives room rates, check-out time, and other details.

As we pass through the door of our lions' den, it's helpful to remember several simple rules which will make our stay easier:

Rule One: Keep doing what got you there in the first place—obeying God.

It's comforting to know that even Jesus, God's perfectly obedient Son, suffered. In fact, His suffering was a necessary part of His ministry:

> For it was fitting for Him, for whom are all things, and through whom are all things, in bringing many sons to glory, to perfect the author of their salvation through sufferings (Hebrews 2:10).

As servants of Christ, we too can expect to suffer and the key to our survival is in responding as our Master did. When Jesus suffered, He did two important things: one, He prayed earnestly; and, two, He called to mind God's Word, putting it into action.

Think for a moment about His temptation by Satan. After His baptism in the Jordan by John, Jesus was led by the Holy Spirit into the wilderness. There He fasted forty days and nights, focusing on His Heavenly Father's will. Then "the tempter came" (Matthew 4:3) and attempted three times to entice Christ into sin:

- He appealed to His hunger, urging Him to use His power selfishly and alleviate it (Matthew 4:3);

- He suggested that Jesus fling Himself off the Temple in Jerusalem, where many would no doubt worship Him as Messiah if He landed unharmed (Matthew 4:6); and,

- He offered Him all the kingdoms of the world— if Christ would worship him (Matthew 4:9).

Each time Satan tempted Jesus, the Lord responded by saying, "It is written . . ." (Matthew 4:4, 7, 10). Christ used "the sword of the Spirit, which is the Word of God" (Ephesians 6:17) to resist the evil one. When we face the lions, we should do the same. It's really the only weapon which will work.

When Daniel was in the lions' den, he may well have quoted Scripture to his roommates. We've already seen that he shut their mouths by faith, and "faith comes from hearing, and hearing by the word . . ." (Romans 10:17)!

Another instance where Christ gave us an example to follow was in Gethsemane, on the eve of His crucifixion. There, "being in agony He was praying very fervently; and His sweat became like drops of blood, falling down upon the ground" (Luke 22:44). Not only did He Himself pray, but He urged the disciples who were with Him to do so:

> *He said to them, "Pray that you may not enter into*
> *temptation"* (Luke 22:40).

The specific issue which sent Daniel to the lions' den was prayer. His longstanding practice was to pray three times daily. He kept praying even after it was outlawed, and he surely must have prayed in the lions' den. We should too. Chances are, if we don't know how to pray before we arrive, we'll certainly learn while we're there!

When we land in the lions' den, we need to follow the examples of both Christ and Daniel and keep doing what got us there in the first place—that is, obeying God. Prayer and the Word of God will sustain us in that difficult hour.

Rule Two: Fix your eyes on Christ.

The Biblical chapter often referred to as faith's "hall of fame"—Hebrews 11—discloses that Daniel shut the lions' mouths by faith, and tells of the righteous acts of other men and women of faith. Then, it's followed by this word of encouragement, which applies not only to believers of the era in which it was written, but also to us:

> *Therefore, since we have so great a cloud of*
> *witnesses surrounding us, let us also lay aside every*
> *encumbrance, and the sin which so easily entangles*
> *us, and let us run with endurance the race that is*

*set before us, fixing our eyes on Jesus, the author
and perfecter of faith, who for the joy set before Him
endured the cross, despising the shame, and has sat
down at the right hand of the throne of God*
(Hebrews 12:1-2).

". . . fixing our eyes on Jesus . . ."

That's an important rule to remember when we're
in the lions' den. In fact, it helped Daniel make it
through that unforgettable night.

"Wait a minute," you say. "Daniel lived some six
centuries before Christ appeared. How could he 'fix his
eyes on Jesus'?"

Granted, Daniel did not see Jesus quite the way we
see Him now, in the light of His first coming. Daniel
saw Him from afar..but he saw Him nonetheless. Several passages of Scripture make this point clear.

Hebrews 11 says that Daniel's forefathers, Abraham
and his descendants,

*died in faith, without receiving the promises, but
having seen them and having welcomed them from a
distance, and having confessed that they were
strangers and exiles on the earth* (verse 13).

Daniel himself knew what it was like to be a stranger
and an exile; he was forced to live most of his life in a
foreign country. The fact that Babylon was not his
home burned in his heart—to such a degree that, as he
prayed three times each day, he did so with his "win-
dows open toward Jerusalem" (Daniel 6:10).

Like his forefathers, Daniel knew that there was
life beyond the borders of Babylon (which happened to

be the region from which Abraham, then known as Abram, had set out to follow God). He was looking for "a better country, that is a heavenly one" (Hebrews 11:16). In other words, Daniel understood that, even if the lions devoured him, a better home, his real home, awaited him in the presence of God.

He also foresaw that Israel's coming Messiah—who was given the name Jesus at birth—would Himself "be cut off and have nothing" (Daniel 9:26). He no doubt figured that if Messiah could be "cut off," then it was a small thing for him to endure suffering and shame for the sake of heaven.

This gave him courage; this gave him heart; this helped see him through the night in the lions' den to the dawning of a new day. It will help us too.

As believers in Jesus Christ, the truth of the matter is that, in a very real sense, we have already died.

> *I have been crucified with Christ,* Paul declared,
> *and it is no longer I who live, but Christ lives in me;*
> *and the life which I now live in the flesh I live by*
> *faith in the Son of God, who loved me, and delivered*
> *Himself up for me* (Galatians 2:20).

Paul wrote to the Christians at Colossae:

> *Set your mind on the things above, not on the things*
> *that are on earth. For you have died and your life is*
> *hidden with Christ in God* (Colossians 3:2-3).

He told the believers at Philippi:

> *For to me, to live is Christ, and to die is gain*
> *(Philippians 1:21).*

Once we have committed our lives to Christ, there's

really nothing this world can do to cause us any ultimate harm. Jesus Himself said:

> And do not fear those who kill the body, but are unable to kill the soul; but rather fear Him who is able to destroy both soul and body in hell (Matthew 10:28).

When Daniel entered the lions' den, he was already a dead man from the world's point of view; in a heavenly sense, however, he was very much alive, and he always would be. The same is true for us when we yield ourselves to God.

By keeping our eyes fixed on Jesus, especially when it seems the lights are about to go out in the lions' den, we can experience glorious freedom—freedom which comes from the knowledge that to be absent from the body is to be at home with the Lord (2 Corinthians 5:8).

Rule Three: Don't lose sight of your friends.

Believe it or not, Daniel still had some friends when he went to the lions' den. One of them was King Darius, whose law was responsible for Daniel's plight!

As soon as Darius learned that he had been manipulated by Daniel's enemies and that Daniel was about to suffer, "he was deeply distressed and set his mind on delivering Daniel; and even until sunset he kept exerting himself to rescue him" (Daniel 6:14).

Even as the law was being enforced and Daniel was being cast into the lions' den, Darius said to Daniel:

> Your God whom you constantly serve will Himself deliver you (Daniel 6:16).

Then, while Daniel was sealed in the lions' den,

the king went off to his palace and spent the night fasting, and no entertainment was brought before him; and his sleep fled from him (Daniel 6:18).

Darius' conduct represents quite a contrast with Belshazzar's, who feasted during the evening prior to his overthrow!

When we wind up in the lions' den, the temptation is for us to think we are all alone in the world, and that nobody else cares.

"Woe is me!" we cry. At such times, however, God Himself is our friend—He sympathizes with our weaknesses (Hebrews 4:15)—and, from His vantage point, we most likely have many other friends.

The Old Testament prophet Elijah was a man who served God mightily, then had to flee for his life. He faced down wicked King Ahab's prophets of Baal at Mount Carmel (see 1 Kings 18), only to find that Jezebel, Ahab's wife, wanted to kill him.

And he was afraid and arose and ran for his life . . . (1 Kings 19:3).

Before long, Elijah was sitting under a juniper tree in the wilderness, asking God to let him die. Instead of taking his life, God sent an angel to strengthen Elijah, who then sought refuge at Mount Horeb. There, the Lord spoke to him:

What are you doing here, Elijah? (1 Kings 19:13).

Elijah replied:

I have been very zealous for the Lord, the God of

hosts; for the sons of Israel have forsaken Thy
covenant, torn down Thine altars and killed Thy
prophets with the sword. And I alone am left; and
they seek my life, to take it away (1 Kings 19:10).

Poor Elijah! What a lonely martyr he was ... at
least until God informed him that He still had 7,000
people in Israel who had not bowed to Baal (1 Kings
19:18).

Daniel still had friends the night he was thrown
into the lions' den. Not only did Darius care about him;
the prophet Ezekiel, a contemporary of Daniel's, respected him too. Ezekiel even recorded that the Lord
had mentioned Daniel to him in the same sentence as
Noah and Job. Those are pretty good character refer-
ences!

What's more, centuries later Daniel received the
ultimate compliment: the Lord Jesus Christ quoted
Daniel's prophecy, referring to him by name (Matthew
24:15).

When we check into the lions' den, it's important for
us to remember that we do still have some friends who
are concerned about us and praying for us. Keeping
this in mind will help prevent us from becoming
depressed and bitter. Paul, who was in prison when he
wrote to the believers at Philippi, experienced this for
himself. To them he declared:

I thank my God in all my remembrance of you, al-
ways offering prayer with joy in my every prayer for
you all, in view of your participation in the gospel
from the first day until now ... I have you in my
heart, since both in my imprisonment and in the

defense and confirmation of the gospel, you all are
partakers of grace with me (Philippians 1:3-5,7).

Not much depression or bitterness there! We too can have joy, even in the lions' den, if we'll remember that we do still have friends—indeed, brothers and sisters in Christ:

A friend loves at all times,
And a brother is born for adversity
(Proverbs 17:17).

Check-Out Time

"All good things must come to an end."

More than once, I've heard others make that statement as vacation drew to a close. It's not true from an eternal standpoint, of course, but it does apply to our experiences in this life. Vacations do end, and the hour does finally arrive to check out of our lodging and go home. Occasionally, it's possible to extend check-out time by an hour or two; but sooner or later, our "home away from home" becomes a memory.

So do our visits to the lions' den.

A more accurate saying spiritually might be, "Suffering gives way to glory." Paul wrote the believers in Rome:

> *For I consider that the sufferings of this present time are not worthy to be compared with the glory that is to be revealed to us* (Romans 8:18).

Peter declared that even the Old Testament prophets, who included Daniel, understood this:

> *As to this salvation, the prophets who prophesied of the grace that would come to you made careful search and inquiry, seeking to know what person or*

*time the Spirit of Christ within them was indicating
as He predicted the sufferings of Christ and the
glories to follow* (1 Peter 1:10-11).

Our risen Lord Himself told the disciples on the
road to Emmaus:

*Was it not necessary for the Christ to suffer these
things and to enter into His glory?* (Luke 24:26).

When we find ourselves in the lions' den, the good
news to bear in mind is that our experience there won't
last forever. We should focus on the good which can be
accomplished in our lives through it and be less concerned about why we are there. Our suffering will give
way to glory. Check-out time will come for us, just as it
did for Daniel.

Daniel's emergence from the lions' den is a dra-
matic, stirring testimony to the faithfulness and power
of Almighty God. Perhaps it is best appreciated from
the perspective of Daniel's friend, King Darius.

As we've pointed out, King Darius was greatly distressed when he learned that Daniel, his faithful servant and counselor, had been trapped by his enemies.
How his stomach must have churned as "a stone was
brought and laid over the mouth of the den; and the
king sealed it with his own signet ring" (Daniel 6:17).
How the hours must have crept by as he "spent the
night fasting, and no entertainment was brought before him; and his sleep fled from him" (Daniel 6:18).

Finally, morning came. Darius knew what the lions
did to people, and he could hardly bear the thought
that righteous Daniel might now be just a bloody,

mangled heap of remains by which the lions sat, licking their fangs.

> *Then the king arose with the dawn, at the break of day, and went in haste to the lions' den. And when he had come near the den to Daniel, he cried out with a troubled voice . . .* (Daniel 6:19-20a).

Let me pause to urge you to put yourself into the picture and grasp the scene by the lions' den early that morning. Too often, we read Scripture in such a hurry that we miss some of the deeply poignant moments recorded there. Fix in your mind the sight of King Darius hurrying toward the den, looking weary and anguished after his sleepless night. Smell with him the sickly scent of the lions as he draws near their den. Hear him as his tortured voice cries out:

> *Daniel, servant of the living God, has your God, whom you constantly serve, been able to deliver you from the lions?* (Daniel 6:20b).

The instant of silence which followed must have seemed like eternity to Darius. Would a man's voice reply, or would he hear only the low, satisfied snarl of the lions?

"O king, live forever!"

The Bible doesn't say how many people were on hand when "Daniel spoke to the king" (Daniel 6:21). There must have been a collective gasp of amazement, however—one like you hear in the Olympics when an athlete performs some unprecedented feat. Daniel had indeed been spared, and he told how:

> *My God sent His angel and shut the lions' mouths,*

and they have not harmed me, inasmuch as I was
found innocent before Him; and also toward you,
O king, I have committed no crime (Daniel 6:22).

What follows next is something of an understate-
ment:

Then the king was very pleased and gave orders for
Daniel to be taken up out of the den. So Daniel was
taken up out of the den, and no injury whatever was
found on him, because he had trusted in his God
(Daniel 6:23).

Daniel's deliverance even resulted in Darius' issuing a
proclamation "to all the peoples, nations, and men of
every language who were living in all the land":

May your peace abound! I make a decree that in all
the dominion of my kingdom men are to fear and
tremble before the God of Daniel;
For He is the living God and enduring forever,
And His kingdom is one which will not be de-
stroyed,
And His dominion will be forever.
He delivers and rescues and performs signs and
wonders
In heaven and on earth,
Who has also delivered Daniel from the power of the
lions (Daniel 6:25-27).

Before pressing on to watch the lions being fed, the
details of this incident force a comparison. Think for a
moment:

. . . a stone . . .

. . . a seal . . .

. . . morning . . .

... a troubled person hurrying toward a tomb ...

... one who should be dead, alive instead—
and speaking ...

... an angel ...

CHRIST'S RESURRECTION!

In a profound way, Daniel's experience in the lions' den foreshadowed the death, burial and resurrection of Jesus Christ. Note the New Testament account of that event:

> *And Joseph took the body and wrapped it in a clean linen cloth, and laid it in his own new tomb, which he had hewn out in the rock; and they rolled a large stone against the entrance of the tomb and went away* (Matthew 27:60).

Next day, the chief priests and the Pharisees, mindful of Jesus' prediction that He would be resurrected, approached Pilate and asked him to secure the grave until the third day, so Jesus' disciples could not steal the body and falsely claim that He had risen.

> *Pilate said to them, "You have a guard; go, make it as secure as you know how." And they went and made the grave secure, and along with the guard they set a seal on the stone* (Matthew 27:65-66).

Then,

> *as it began to dawn toward the first day of the week, Mary Magdalene and the other Mary came to look at the grave* (Matthew 28:1).

They found, however, that

> *a severe earthquake had occurred, for an angel of*

> *the Lord descended from heaven and came and*
> *rolled away the stone and sat upon it*
> (Matthew 28:2).

The angel told them:

> *He is not here, for He has risen, just as He said.*
> *Come, see the place where He was lying*
> (Matthew 28:6).

The two Marys then left "the tomb with fear and great joy and ran to report it to His disciples" (Matthew 28:8).

> *And behold, Jesus met them and greeted them . . .*
> (Matthew 28:9).

At that point, the women must have felt somewhat like Darius when he heard Daniel's voice:

"O king, live forever!"

No wonder—Daniel's deliverance pointed to Christ's resurrection. The Lord must have found comfort in reflecting upon Daniel's experience as He faced the prospect of His own suffering and death. In fact, Daniel's episode with the lions was a demonstration of the relationship with the Lord which Paul wrote about in Philippians 3:7-11:

> *But whatever things were gain to me, those things I*
> *have counted as loss for the sake of Christ. More*
> *than that, I count all things to be loss in view of the*
> *surpassing value of knowing Christ Jesus my Lord,*
> *for whom I have suffered the loss of all things, and*
> *count them but rubbish in order that I may gain*
> *Christ . . . that I may know Him, and the power of*
> *His resurrection and the fellowship of His suffer-*
> *ings, being conformed to His death; in order that I*
> *may attain to the resurrection from the dead.*

One interesting sidelight is that Daniel's reply to Darius—"O king, live forever!"—can be viewed as a prayer for Darius' salvation. How can a man live forever? Jesus said:

> *I am the resurrection and the life; he who believes in Me shall live even if he dies, and everyone who lives and believes in Me shall never die* (John 11:25-26).

What about it, my friend: do you believe in Him? If so, you'll live forever . . . and as a believer, yours is the wondrous privilege of knowing Christ in both the power of His resurrection and the fellowship of His sufferings. Nothing else this world offers can compare with that experience, and with the glory to which it leads when the time comes for you to "check out."

Whatever your lions' den may be, by faith you'll either be delivered from it, to enter the Lord's presence later under other circumstances, or you'll depart through it to be with God Himself. Either way, you'll be able to say with Paul:

> *. . . thanks be to God, who gives us the victory through our Lord Jesus Christ* (2 Corinthians 15:57).

Now, about those lions. They did get their meal after Daniel's departure from the lions' den:

> *The king then gave orders, and they brought those men who had maliciously accused Daniel, and they cast them, their children, and their wives into the lions' den; and they had not reached the bottom of the den before the lions overpowered them and crushed all their bones* (Daniel 6:24).

God's judgment on evil may sometimes seem to be slow in coming, but it does come. When it does, it is sudden, swift and complete. That's why the Psalmist wrote:

> *Do not fret because of evildoers,*
> *Be not envious toward wrongdoers.*
> *For they will wither quickly like the grass,*
> *And fade like the green herb.*
> *Yet a little while and the wicked man will be no*
> *more;*
> *And you will look carefully for his place, and he will*
> *not be there.*
> *But the humble will inherit the land,*
> *And will delight themselves in abundant prosperity*
> (Psalm 37:1-2, 10-11).

When we find ourselves in the lions' den, we need to leave to God the job of judging and punishing those responsible for our plight:

> *Never take your own revenge, beloved, but leave*
> *room for the wrath of God, for it is written,*
> *"Vengeance is Mine, I will repay," says the Lord*
> (Romans 12:19).

Parting Thoughts

Not too long ago, my wife Glenda and I gave our kids, Hannah, Gregory and Nathan, a vacation: she and I spent several days together in the southwestern United States while they stayed with grandparents in North Carolina. (It's a tough job, but somebody has to do it!) Glenda and I had a fun time, and we took lots of photos to remind ourselves of our—I mean, our kids' break from the routine. Even now, we enjoy looking at those pictures and savoring the sights and experiences we shared.

Long after you and I check out of the lions' den, we'll surely reflect on it every now and then. Even though it was no resort hotel, we'll realize that God is faithful and that our stay in the lions' den left us with lasting benefits in many areas of our lives.

As I think about Daniel's experience, a number of thoughts come to mind about its lessons for Christians in these last years of this millenium:

Concerning angels.

Not too many years ago in our society, it seemed only "ignorant" people believed in the reality of anything which couldn't be seen, touched, tasted or measured. Nowadays, public figures talk openly about their belief in, and experiences with, the unseen or "spiritual" world. Many attest to personal encounters and even ongoing relationships with spirit-beings. My, how things have changed!

We as God's people should expect to experience the ministry of angels in our lives. Why? Because they are

> *ministering spirits, sent out to render service for the*
> *sake of those who will inherit salvation*
> (Hebrews 1:14).

God has always used angels to perform assigned tasks in our world. Scripture is full of their acts. Angels delivered messages and, as we have seen, strengthened and safeguarded God's servants. They were instrumental in Israel's deliverance from slavery in Egypt; in preserving Shadrach, Meshach and Abednego in the fiery furnace, and Daniel in the lions' den; and in freeing Peter from jail, to cite just a few random examples. We should not be surprised when angels undertake for us in this day and time.

Angels are not usually visible to us, but that does not mean they are not working on our behalf. I liken angels to the housekeeping and security staff in a hotel; I often don't see them as they go about their duties, but their jobs get done nonetheless.

When we enter our own lions' dens, we should take comfort in the promise of God's Word:

> *For He will give His angels charge concerning you,*
> *To guard you in all your ways.*

They will bear you up in their hands,
Lest you strike your foot against a stone.
You will tread upon the lion and cobra,
The young lion and the serpent you will
trample down
(Psalm 91:11-13).

Concerning job performance.

All my adult life, it has been my privilege to be involved in vocational Christian service. In other words, I spend my time spreading the gospel, and in the process, receive the financial support necessary for me and my family. This is both Biblical and honorable:

So also the Lord directed those who proclaim the
gospel to get their living from the gospel
(1 Corinthians 9:14).

I realize, however, that you and most others who read this book may not get your living from the gospel. Certainly you too are involved in spreading the Good News, but your paycheck comes from your work as a salesperson, secretary, attorney, mechanic, doctor, teacher, banker or whatever else you happen to do.

Know what? Both of us have an obligation in our jobs to be like Daniel—not negligent or corrupt, but faithful and excellent. We should turn in the very best performance we can, day after day. Why? To reflect positively on the God to whom we belong.

Daniel did not use the fact that he was a captive in pagan surroundings a long way from home as an excuse to slack off. Even when we find ourselves in job environments which are difficult, we too should seek to

live distinctively. Others will notice, and so will the
Lord:

> *Whatever you do, do your work heartily, as for the*
> *Lord rather than for men; knowing that from the*
> *Lord you will receive the reward of the inheritance.*
> *It is the Lord Christ whom you serve*
> (Colossians 3:24).

Concerning our families.

To me, one of the tragedies of Daniel six is that the
families of Daniel's wicked enemies also became lion
bait. After all, it was the husbands, not the wives and
children, who plotted against Daniel. These innocent
victims suffered because of their husbands' and fathers'
actions.

Eternally, God is just and each person is responsible for his or her own choices and actions. In this life,
however, the fact is that the individuals closest to us do
suffer or prosper as a result of our choices. Kids suffer
when their parents are dishonest or financially irre-
sponsible or sexually unfaithful to each other. Parents
suffer when their children use drugs or become involved
in other destructive activities. Choices in life are ours
to make, but we must always bear in mind that others
will be affected by them.

Maybe right now, you are considering a course of
action which, if taken, will bring great suffering and
heartache to those around you. Whatever your situation, please, make the right choice—for the sake of
your family as well as yourself. Ask God to help you do
what is right, and obey the principles of wholesome

living clearly set forth in His Word:

> *For the commandment is a lamp, and the teaching*
> *is light; And reproofs for discipline are the way of*
> *life* (Proverbs 6:23).

Think of Daniel and his enemies. Daniel did not take the easy road through life, yet he emerged triumphant. His enemies took the selfish path, leading to the destruction of themselves and their loved ones.

Concerning civil disobedience.

No one in Babylon was a more responsible citizen than Daniel. If Daniel lived in America today, he would pay his full share of taxes, vote, observe the speed limit, and refrain from littering. He would likely receive recognition for his contribution to the community.

It may well be that he would also end up in jail—not for any negligence or corruption, but for the sake of his conscience. While Daniel distinguished himself as a servant of the king in Babylon, issues did arise in which he could not, before God, go with the program. In those matters, he sought to work constructively within the system to bring about change. He was a skillful diplomat, as was shown by his successful effort to avoid eating the unlawful foods prescribed by the king.

When he could not work within the system to effect changes he could live with, though, he was not afraid to disobey, even when it meant going to the lions' den.

I love our country and thank God for the freedoms we enjoy and the privileges of living here. I'm deeply saddened, however, that our society seems to be increasingly characterized, even in its laws, by ungodly practices. You and I should work within the system, as far as we possibly can, to change those practices which conflict with God's Word and disturb our conscience. This means choosing carefully and wisely the strategies by which we resist evil.

On the other hand, when we have no more options left for pursuing change, we must not flinch if being faithful means that we too go to the lions' den. Like Daniel,

> here we do not have a lasting city, but we are
> seeking the city which is to come (Hebrews 13:14).

One day soon, our Lord and Savior Jesus Christ will return to this earth to establish His kingdom of righteousness. Satan will be "thrown into the lake of fire and brimstone" (Revelation 20:10). The lions which roar and threaten us now will be stilled. In that day,

> the wolf will dwell with the lamb,
> And the leopard will lie down with the kid,
> And the calf and the young lion and the fatling
> together;
> And a little boy will lead them.
> Also the cow and the bear will graze;
> Their young will lie down together;
> And the lion will eat straw like the ox
> (Isaiah 11:6-7).

What matters most in this world is that we be ready for that time. The way to prepare is to entrust our lives to Jesus Christ now, then take those three important steps, so clearly modeled for us by Daniel:

1. A commitment to holiness;

2. A commitment to truth; and,

3. A commitment to a transformed lifestyle.

If we'll do those things, then we, like Daniel, will see Him who said:

> *Behold, I am coming quickly, and My reward is with Me, to render to every man according to what he has done* (Revelation 22:12).

About *AWAKENINGS*

AWAKENINGS, INCORPORATED is an interdenominational, non-profit ministry of evangelism and discipleship based in Winston-Salem, North Carolina. *AWAKENINGS* was founded in 1989 for the purpose of communicating God's Word, and helping others do so worldwide. *AWAKENINGS* is committed to:

- Guiding individuals into a Biblical relationship with Jesus Christ;

- Helping Christians understand and apply the Bible; and

- Equipping churches to reach out effectively and make disciples.

AWAKENINGS conducts conferences, retreats and special services at the invitation of local churches, and produces Bible-based study materials aimed at strengthening Christ's Body.

Individuals interested in additional information about *AWAKENINGS* or in scheduling an *AWAKENINGS* representative for a specific ministry opportunity are invited to call or write. Also, financial support for the ministry of *AWAKENINGS* is tax-deductible and may be sent to the following address:

> *AWAKENINGS, INCORPORATED*
> Post Office Box 25251
> Winston-Salem, NC 27114-5251
> Telephone (919) 765-9392